PIANO/VOCAL/GUITAR + AUDIO DOWNLOAD

RICHARD O'BRIEN'S

THE ROCKY HORROR SHOW

40TH ANNIVERSARY SONGBOOK

HAL•LEONARD®

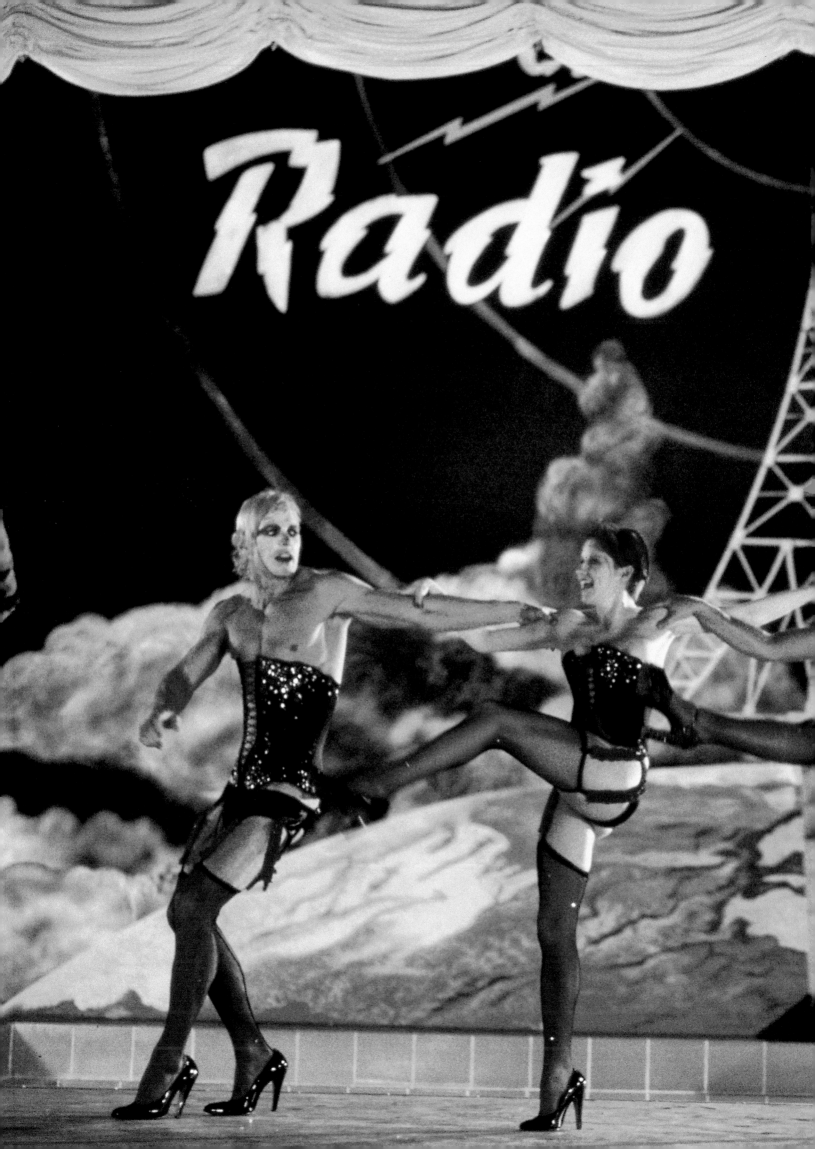

Exclusive Distributors:
Contact us:
Hal Leonard
7777 West Bluemound Road, Milwaukee, WI 53213
Email: info@halleonard.com

In Europe, contact:
Hal Leonard Europe Limited
1 Red Place, London W1K 6PL
Email: info@halleonardeurope.com

In Australia, contact:
Hal Leonard Australia Pty. Ltd.
4 Lentara Court, Cheltenham, Victoria 9132, Australia
Email: info@halleonard.com.au

ISBN: 978-1-78305-149-6

Music and lyrics © Druidcrest Ltd.

Edited by Jenni Norey.
Colour photographs by Mick Rock of the cast
of the Rocky Horror Picture Show.
Other images courtesy of the composer.

With thanks to Richard O'Brien, Andy Leighton,
Stanley Banks and Julian Lyons.

Backing tracks match the 1990 cast recording.
Audio Mixed and mastered by Jonas Persson and John Rose.
Piano and keyboards by Paul Honey.
Guitars by Arthur Dick.
Bass by Don Richardson.
Drums by Chris Baron.

BACK IN NINETEEN FIFTYEIGHT, WHEN I WAS SUPPOSED TO BE AT NIGHTSCHOOL STUDYING ART, THE NIGHTS WERE WARM AND THE CLASS WAS BORING SO I'D STOP OFF AT THE LATE-SHOW WHICH WAS ALWAY DOUBLE FEATURE...HERE AMONGST THE OTHER DELINQUENTS, PARADISE WAS TO BE MINE..."HORROR ON THE CAMPUS"AND..."I WAS A TEEN-AGED WEREWOLF' ...WERE VERY WELL RECIEVED, FOURTEEN YEARS LATER I WAS SITTING ONE EVENING WITH MY FRIEND JOHN SINCLAIR, WHO HAS SINCE BECOME A SUCCESSFUL RECORD PRODUCER SINCE,(AND TO THINK I KNEW HIM WHEN HE WAS SOMEBODY) AND WE DISCUSSED THE THOUGHT OF WRITING A SHOW THAT WE OURSELVES WOULD LIKE TO GO AND SEE...WE WERE TO WRITE IT TOGETHER...IT WAS TO BE A COLLECTION OF ALL THE THINGS GIVE YOU A BUZZ...LET'S DO IT SAID JOHN AND PROMPTLY WENT OFF TO OPEN SAM A RECORDING STUDIOS...JILTED, I SAT AT HOME NIGHTS WRITING SONGS AND BITS OF DIOLOGUE...SOME FOUR MONTHS LATER I HAD THE GOOD LUCK TO BE WORKING WITH JIM SHARMAN AND BRIAN THOMSON, THE TWO AUSTALIAN WIZARDS WHO MADE "JESUS CHRIST SUPERSTAR"A STAGE HIT IN LONDON AND AUSTRALIA...THE PLAY WE WERE TO DO WAS CALLED "THE UNSEEN HAND" WRITTEN BY THE GREAT SAM SHEPARD...I WAS TO PLAY WILLIE THE SPACE FREAK.

    DURING REHEARSALS I MENTIONED TO JIM AND BRIAN THAT I WAS WRITING A ROCK-HORROR MUSICAL THAT WAS AMUSING ME AND I ADDED THAT IT MIGHT DO THE SAME FOR THEM....I HAD NO DOUBT ABOUT THEIR TALENT...I KNEW THEY THOUGHT I WAS ALRIGHT BECAUSE THEY'D CAST ME IN THE PLAY WE WERE DOING...UNABASHED NAIVETY IS A STRONG SELLING POINT....(ONCE)

    ONE FATEFUL NIGHT AFTER A REHEARSAL, DIRECTOR JIM, DRAGGED RICHARD HARTLEY WHO WAS WORKING ON SOME TOONS FOR US IN UNSEEN HAND, BACK TO MY PLACE....RICHARD WAS ENTHUSIASTIC IN THE CAB, I REMEMBER HIM SAYING, "OH NO NOT ANOTHER ROCK-MUSICAL"...SO THERE I WAS, WITH MY SCRIBBLED FEW PAGES AND A MUCH LOVED LEVIN GUITAR, ON TRIAL...I SANG THE OPENING SONG, "SCIENCE FICTION" AND I BLUSH TO RELATE THIS, BUT I WAS MADE TO SING IT FOR TWO MORE TIMES THERE AND THEN, AND WHEN I'D FINISHED THE(THEN) SLENDER SCRIPT I HAD TO SING THAT SONG AGAIN....
WE OPENED FOR A FIVE WEEK SEASON AT "THE THEATRE UPSTAIRS" AT "THE ROYAL COURT" , AND THANKS TO THE BRILLIANCE OF THE CAST...SUE BLANE'S COSTUME DESIGNS...BRIAN THOMSONS... SET...RICHARD HARTLEY'S ARRANGEMENTS AND JIM SHARMANS DIRECTION...WE WERE A SELL-OUT AND THE REST IS HISTORY..

    MY THANKS TO ALL THOSE THAT GET OFF ON THE SHOW ARE UNLIMITED...THERE IS NO DOUBT IN MY MIND, THAT ROCKY FREAKS ARE THE SANEST MADMEN IN THE WORLD...OTHER PLANETS ??¢?8?? WELL......THAT'S PRIVILEDGED INFORMATION.

YOURS UNTIL THEY COME TO TAKE US AWAY,

THE ROCKY HORROR SHOW by Richard O'Brien

KING'S ROAD THEATRE
THE ROCKY HORROR SHOW by Richard O'Brien

KINGS ROAD THEATRE
THE ROCKY HORROR SHOW

AWARDS

in the presence of
H.R.H. PRINCESS ALEXANDRA

•

Most Outstanding Achievement
in Opera
REGINALD GOODALL

•

Most Outstanding Achievement
in Ballet
CHRISTOPHER BRUCE

•

Best Play of the Year
SATURDAY, SUNDAY, MONDAY
Eduardo de Filippo

•

Best Performance by an Actress
JANET SUZMAN

•

Best Performance by an Actor
ALEC McCOWEN

•

Best Musical of the Year
ROCKY HORROR SHOW

•

Most Promising Playwright
DAVID WILLIAMSON
for "The Removalists"

•

Best Comedy of the Year
ABSURD PERSON SINGULAR
Alan Ayckbourn

Special Award
LORD OLIVIER
Director of the National Theatre.
1963-1973

CHAIRMAN
Sir Max Aitken
Chairman of Beaverbrook Newspapers

TOAST TO THE ARTS
proposed by
Norman St. John Stevas, MP
Minister for the Arts

Mr. Charles Wintour
Editor of the Evening Standard

LET'S DO, THE.....
TIME WARP
BASIC STEPS

1 (ITS JUST A) JUMP TO THE LEFT, WITH HANDS UP
2 A STEP TO THE RIGHT (TIME-WARPER ANNETTE FUNICELLO
   SUGGESTS A VERY WIDE STEP.)
3* (WITH YOUR HANDS ON YOUR HIPS)
   YOU BRING YOUR KNEES IN TIGHT.
4 (THEN) THE PELVIC THRUST (IF REPEATED FIVE TIMES, IT
   NEARLY DRIVES YOU INSA-A-ANE)
5 HIPSWIVEL (IF NOT DRIVEN INSA-A-ANE BY STEP FOUR)
6 LET'S DO THE TIME WARP AGAIN!!
* THOSE WITH LIMB DISABILITIES MAY FIND IT NECESSARY
   TO ALTER OR DELETE THIS ACTION, BUT NO EXCUSES
   FOR ALTERATIONS TO STEPS FOUR AND FIVE.

SCIENCE FICTION – DOUBLE FEATURE

WORDS & MUSIC BY RICHARD O'BRIEN

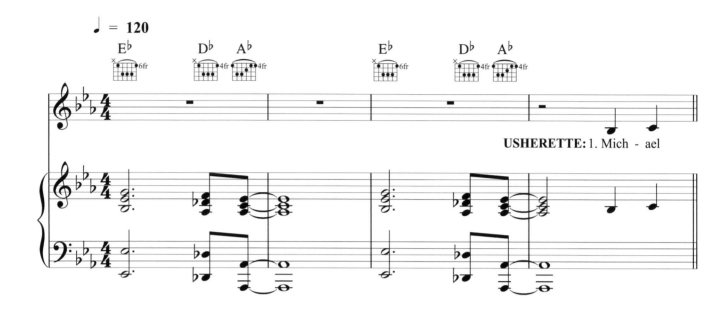

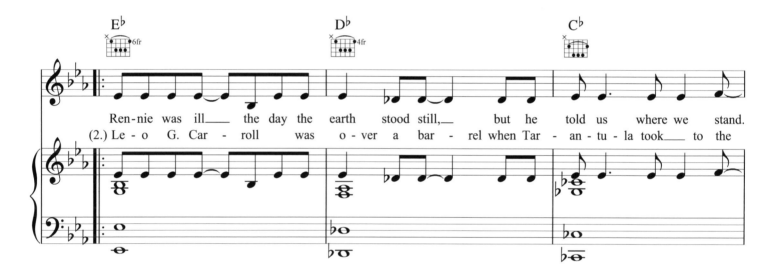

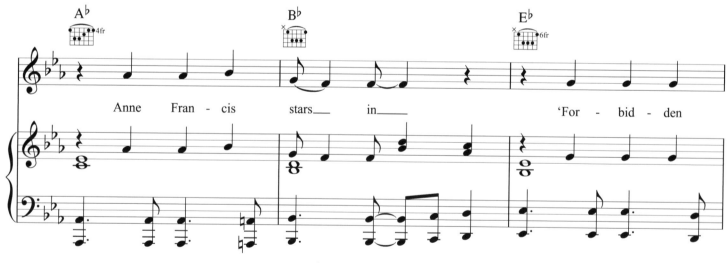

late night, dou - ble fea - ture pic - ture show.

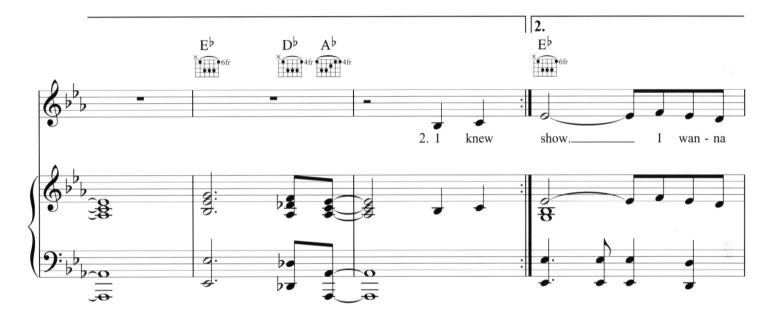

2. I knew show._____ I wan - na

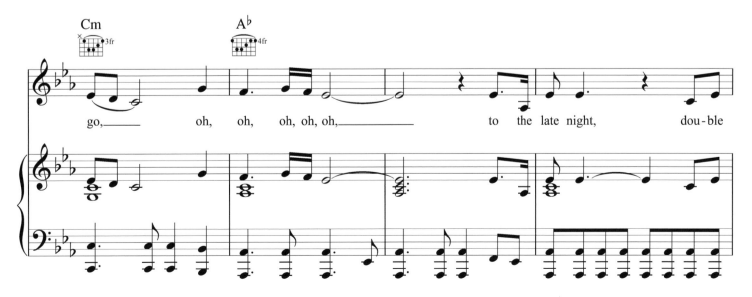

go,_____ oh, oh, oh, oh, oh,_____ to the late night, dou - ble

DAMMIT JANET

WORDS & MUSIC BY RICHARD O'BRIEN

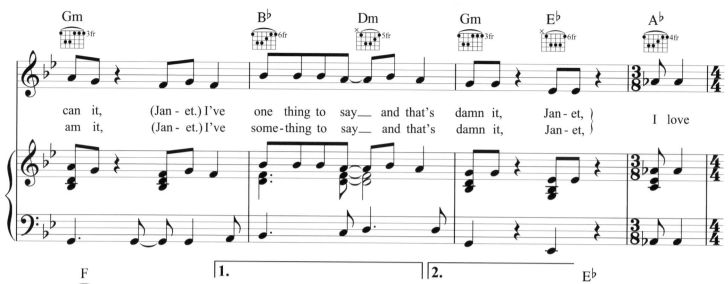

can it, (Jan-et.) I've one thing to say__ and that's damn it, Jan-et,
am it, (Jan-et.) I've some-thing to say__ and that's damn it, Jan-et,
I love

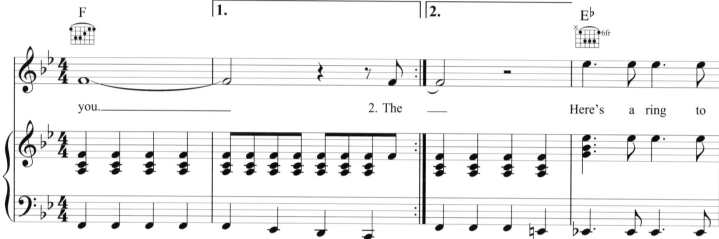

you._____ 2. The __ Here's a ring to

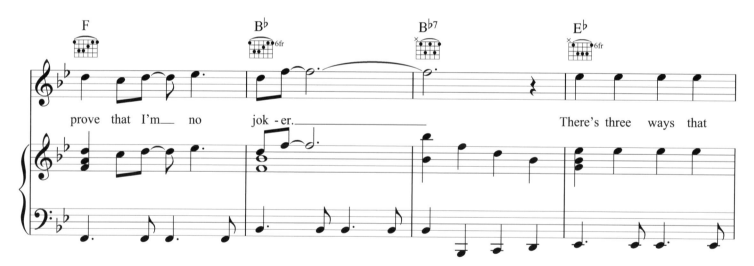

prove that I'm__ no jok-er._____ There's three ways that

love__ can grow,_____ that's good,

bad   or   me - di - o - cre._____ Oh,

J A N E T I love you so._____ 3. Oh! It's

nic-er than Bet - ty Mun - ro had, (Oh Brad.)   now we're en - gaged and I'm   so glad, (Oh Brad.)
(4.) go see the man that be - gan it, (Jan - et.) when we met in his sci - ence ex - am, it (Jan - et.) made me

that you met mum and you know___ dad, (Oh Brad.) I've one thing to say___ and that's Brad I'm mad
give you the eye and then___ pan - ic, (Jan - et.) I've one thing to say___ and that's damn it, Jan - et,

To Coda ⊕

20

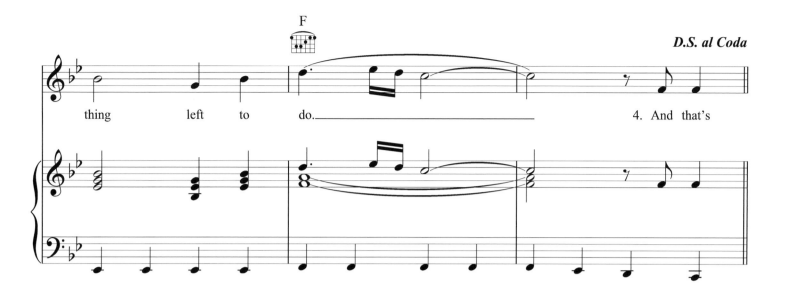

thing   left   to   do._____   4. And   that's

Coda

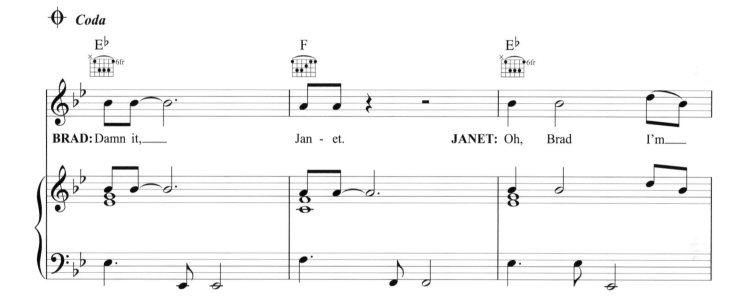

BRAD: Damn it,____   Jan - et.   **JANET:** Oh,   Brad   I'm___

rit.

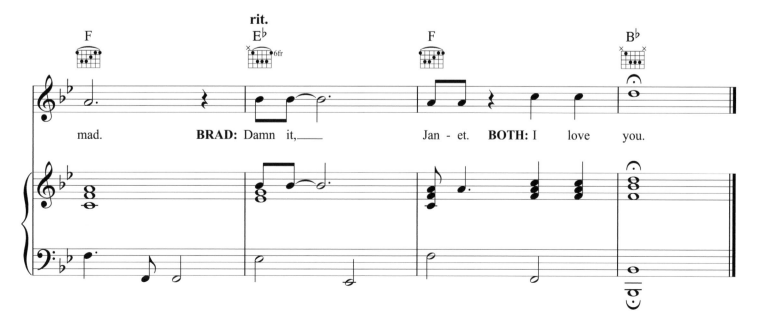

mad.   **BRAD:** Damn it,____   Jan - et.   **BOTH:** I   love   you.

OVER AT THE FRANKENSTEIN PLACE

WORDS & MUSIC BY RICHARD O'BRIEN

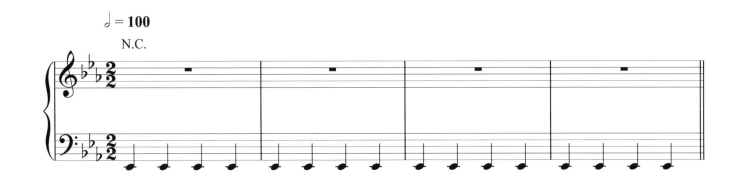

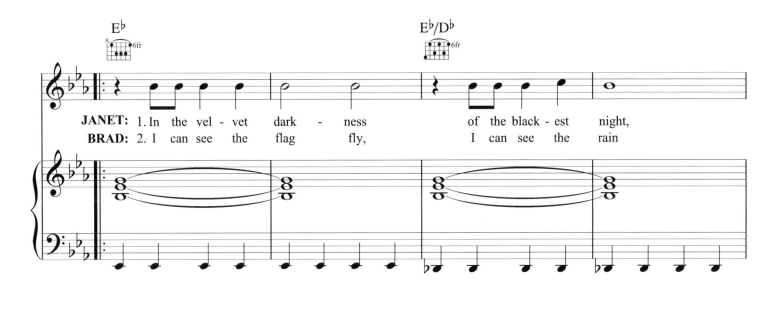

JANET: 1. In the vel - vet dark - ness of the black - est night,

BRAD: 2. I can see the flag fly, I can see the rain

burn - ing bright, there's a guid - ing

just the same, there has got to

star,_____ no mat- ter
be,_____ some-thing bet- ter

what or_____ who you
here for_____ you and

are._____ BOTH: There's a
me._____

light_____ o- ver at the Fran-ken-stein

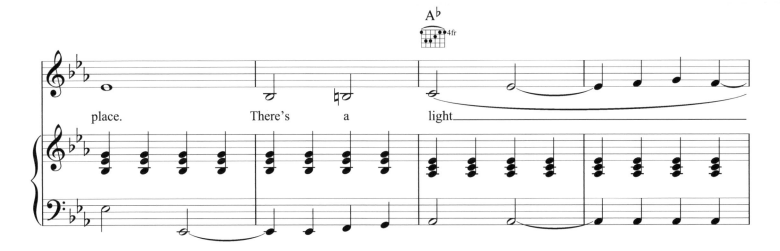

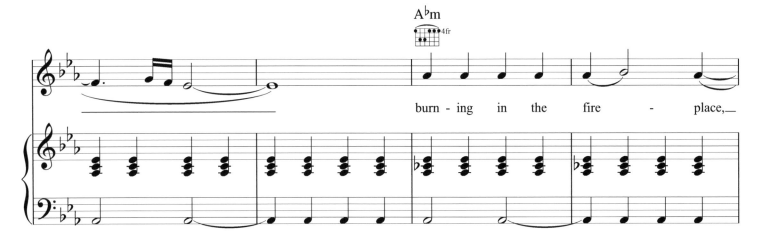

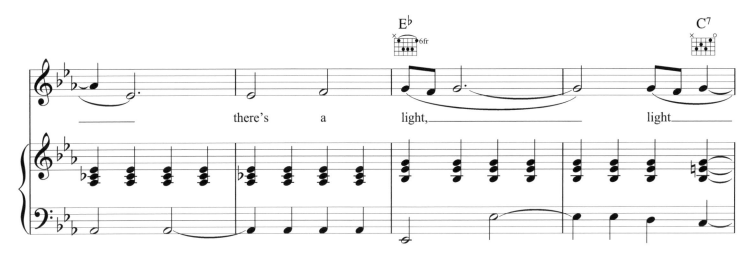

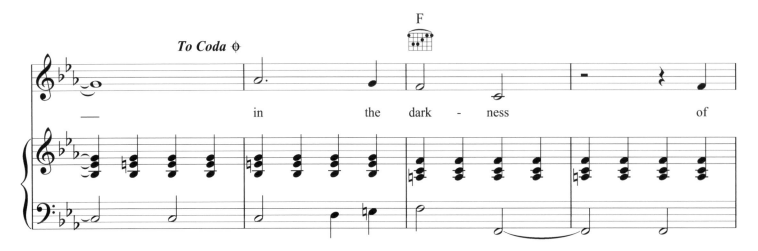

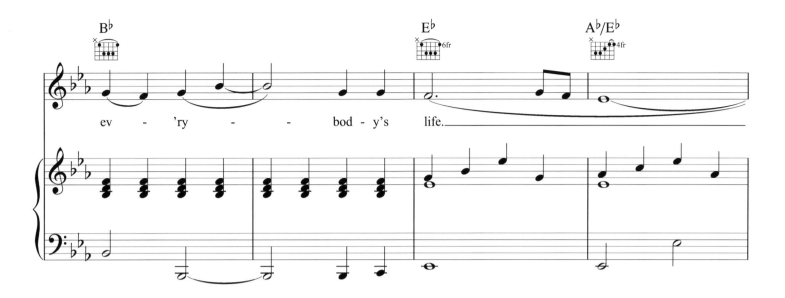

ev - 'ry - - bod - y's life.___

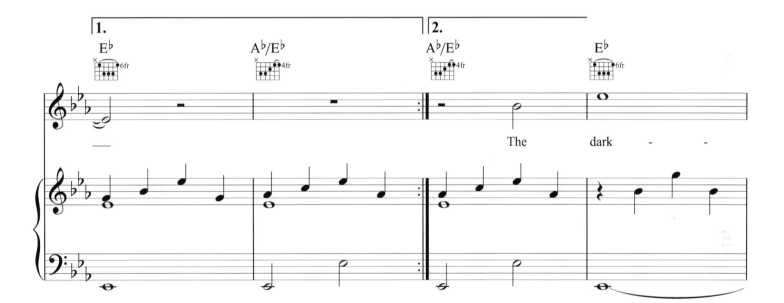

The dark - -

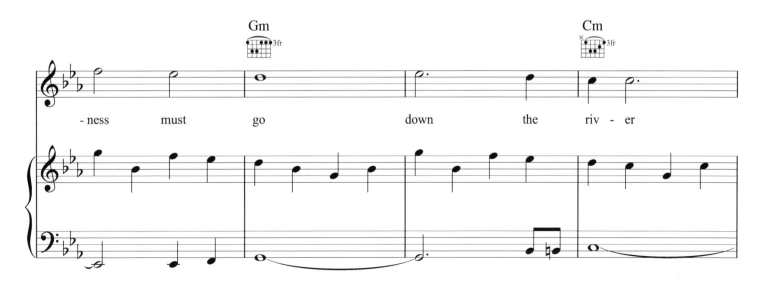

-ness must go down the riv - er

of night's dream - ing._____ Flow

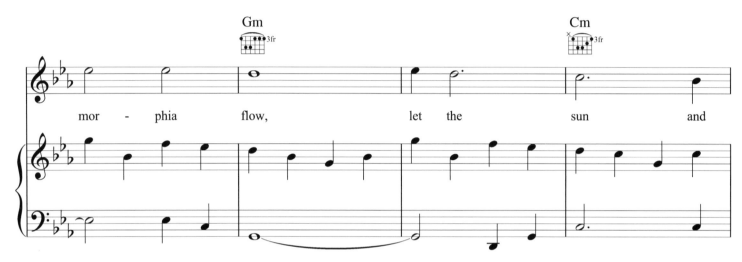

mor - phia flow, let the sun and

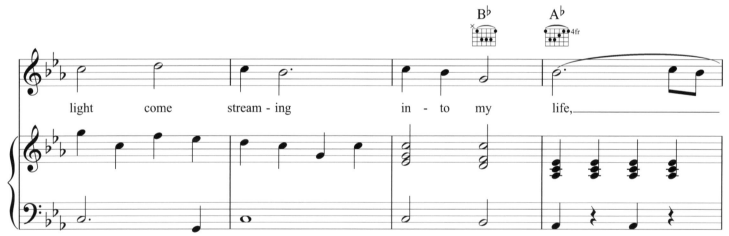

light come stream - ing in - to my life,_____

_____ in - to my life,_____

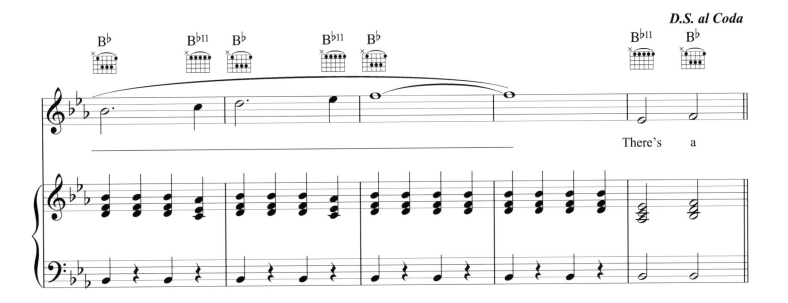

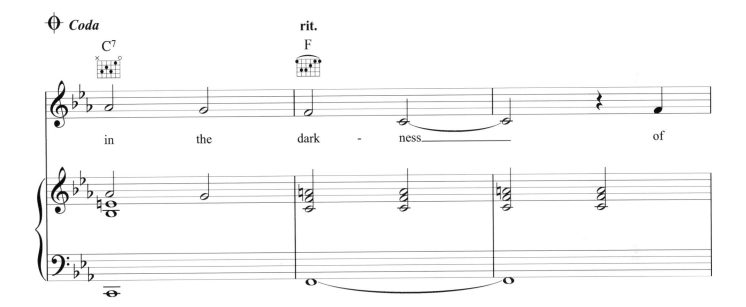

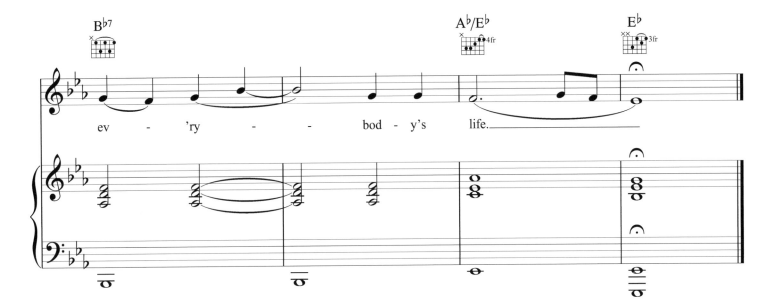

THE TIME WARP

WORDS & MUSIC BY RICHARD O'BRIEN

with your hands on your hips,___ you bring your knees_ in tight,___

but it's the pel - vic thrust,___ that real-ly drives you in - sane.___

Let's do the Time Warp a - gain,___

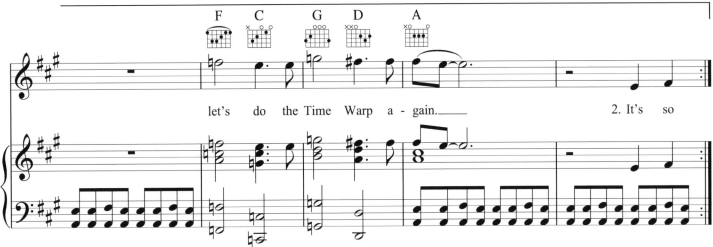

let's do the Time Warp a - gain.___ 2. It's so

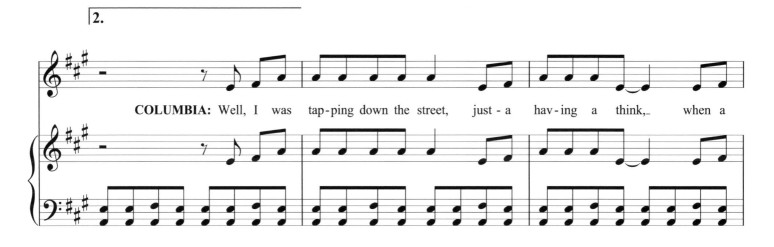

COLUMBIA: Well, I was tap-ping down the street, just-a hav-ing a think,__ when a

snake of a guy__ gave me an e-vil wink,__ it shook me up,__ it took me

by sur-prise,__ had a pick-up truck__ and the dev-il's eyes.__ He

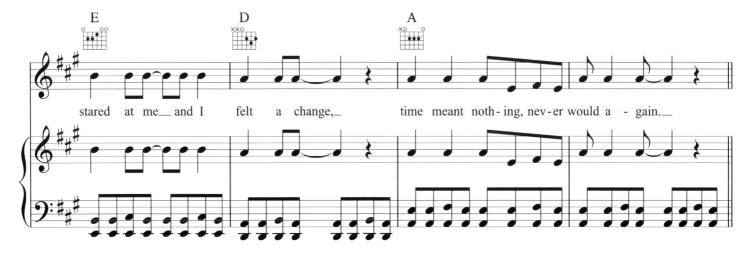

stared at me__ and I felt a change,__ time meant noth-ing, nev-er would a - gain.__

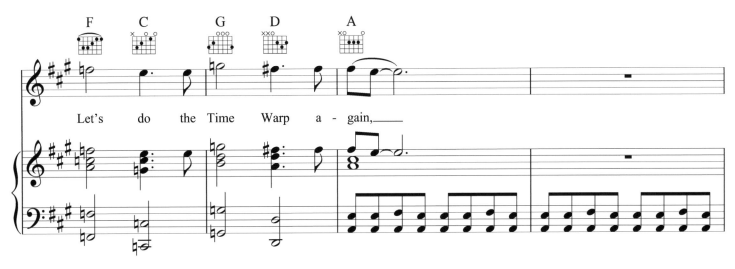

Let's do the Time Warp a-gain,

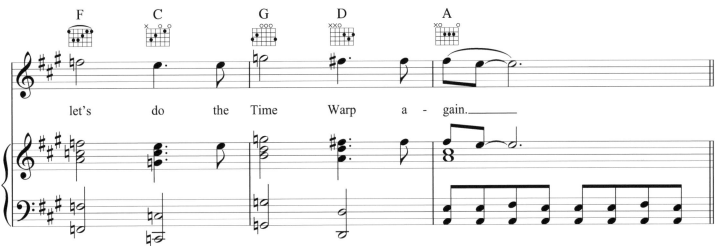

let's do the Time Warp a-gain.

It's just a jump to the left,___ and then a step to the right,___

with your hands on your hips,___ you bring your knees___ in

tight,_____ but it's the pel - vic thrust,_____

that real - ly drives you in - sane._____

Let's do the Time Warp a - gain,_____

let's do the Time Warp a - gain._____

34

THE SWORD OF DAMOCLES

WORDS & MUSIC BY RICHARD O'BRIEN

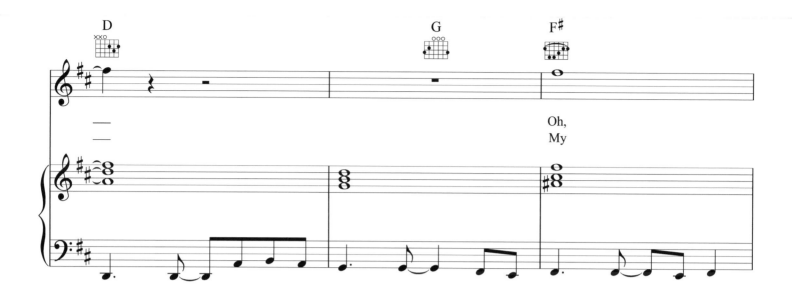

Oh,
My

woe is me,___ my life___ is a mis-er-y,___
high is low,___ I'm dressed up with no place to go

oh oh___ can't you see___ that I'm at the start of a
and all I know___ is I'm at the start of a

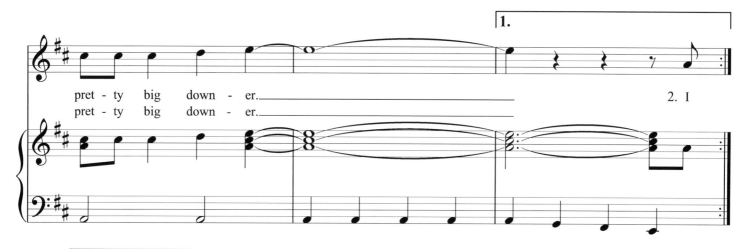

pret - ty big down - er._____ 2. I

pret - ty big down - er._____

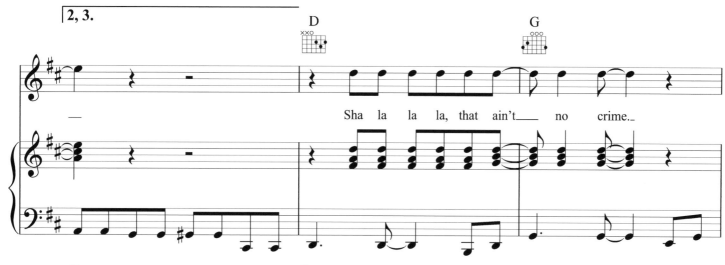

Sha la la la, that ain't___ no crime._

Sha la la la, that ain't___ no crime.____ Sha la la la, that ain't_

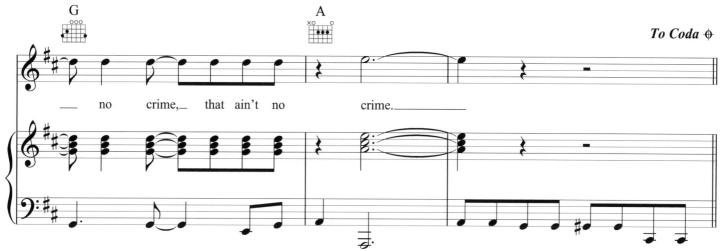

To Coda ⊕

__ no crime,_ that ain't no crime._____

Rock - y Hor - ror you need peace of mind,___

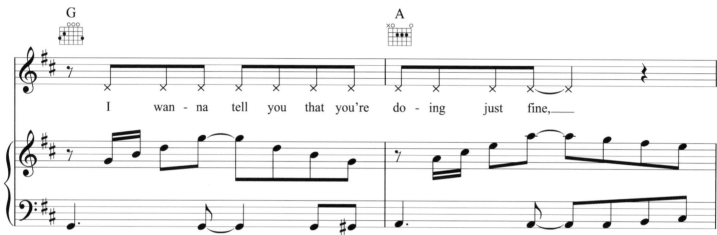

I wan - na tell you that you're do - ing just fine,___

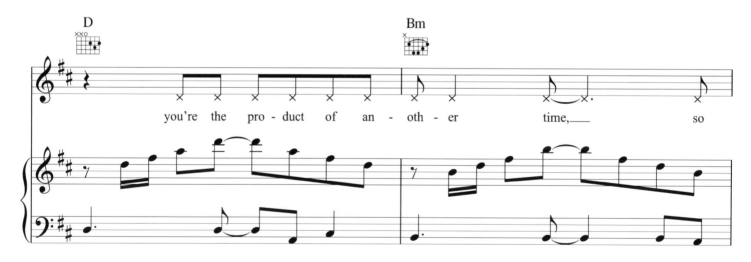

you're the pro - duct of an - oth - er time,___ so

feel - ing low,___ well that's no crime.___

SWEET TRANSVESTITE

WORDS & MUSIC BY RICHARD O'BRIEN

look like you're both pret-ty groo-vy. But if you want some-thing vis-ual that's
I could show you my fav-'rite ob-ses-sion. I've been mak-ing a man

1.

not too a-bys-mal, we could take in an old Steve Reeves mov-ie.
with blonde hair and a tan and he's good for re-liev-ing my

2.

ten-sion. I'm just a sweet trans-ves-tite from Trans-sex-ual,

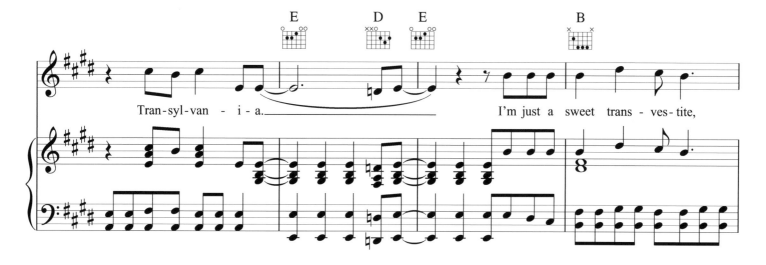

Tran-syl-van - i - a._____ I'm just a sweet trans-ves-tite,

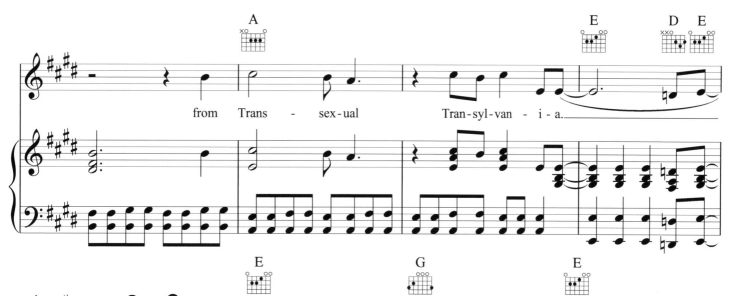

from Trans - sex-ual Tran-syl-van - i - a._____

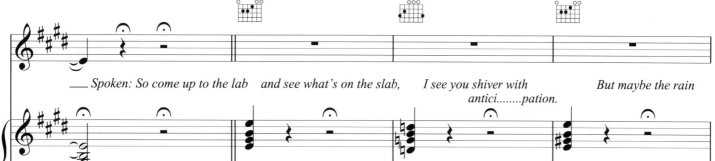

_____ Spoken: So come up to the lab and see what's on the slab, I see you shiver with
antici........pation. But maybe the rain

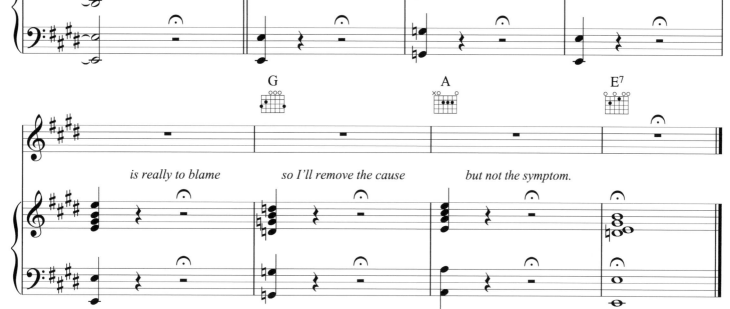

is really to blame so I'll remove the cause but not the symptom.

I CAN MAKE YOU A MAN

WORDS & MUSIC BY RICHARD O'BRIEN

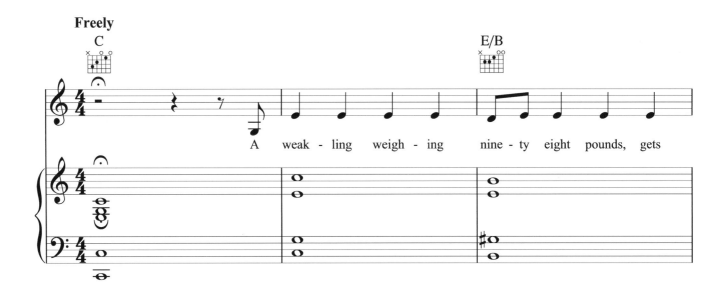

A weak-ling weigh-ing nine-ty eight pounds, gets

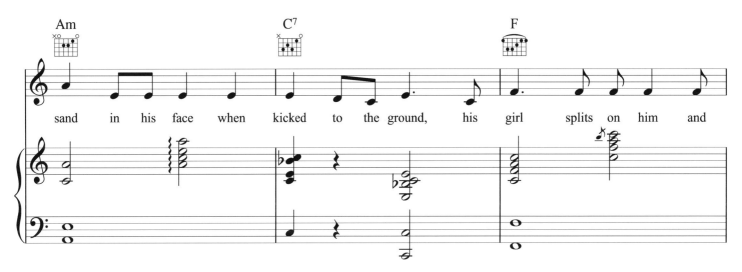

sand in his face when kicked to the ground, his girl splits on him and

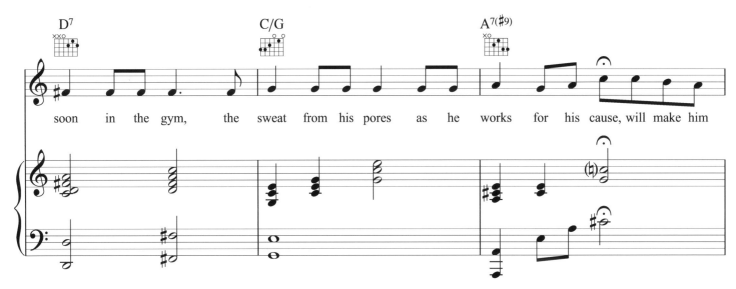

soon in the gym, the sweat from his pores as he works for his cause, will make him

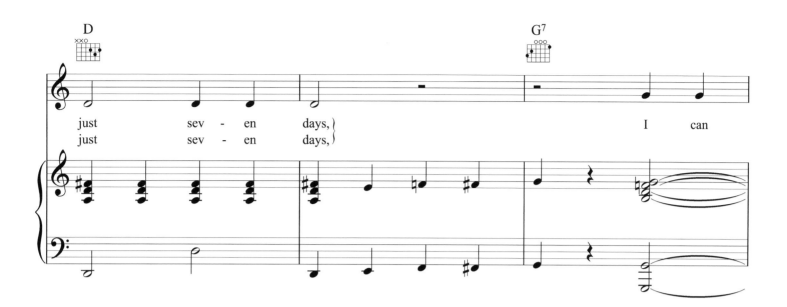

just sev - en days,⎱ I can
just sev - en days,⎰

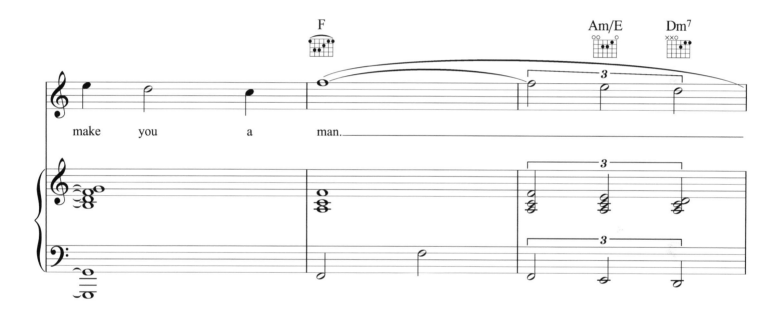

make you a man.

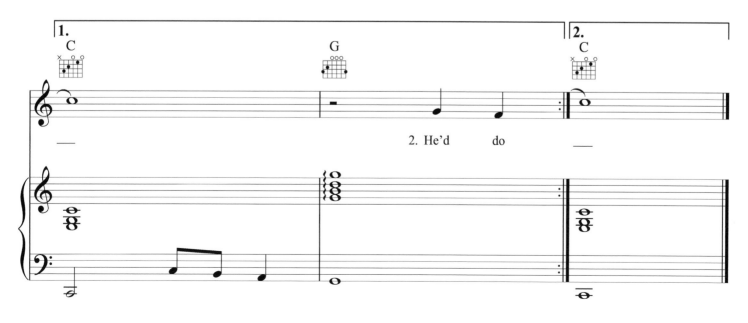

2. He'd do

HOT PATOOTIE – BLESS MY SOUL

WORDS & MUSIC BY RICHARD O'BRIEN

climbed in the back___ and you real - ly had a good time, yeah._____
felt pret - ty good___ 'cause you real - ly had a good time._____

Hot pa - too - tie,   bless my soul,___   I real - ly love that

rock and roll.___   Hot pa - too - tie,   bless my soul,___

I real - ly love that rock and roll.____

⊕ *Coda*

Hot pa - too - tie bless my soul,____ I real - ly love that

1.

rock and roll.____

2.

rock and roll.____

I CAN MAKE YOU A MAN: REPRISE

WORDS & MUSIC BY RICHARD O'BRIEN

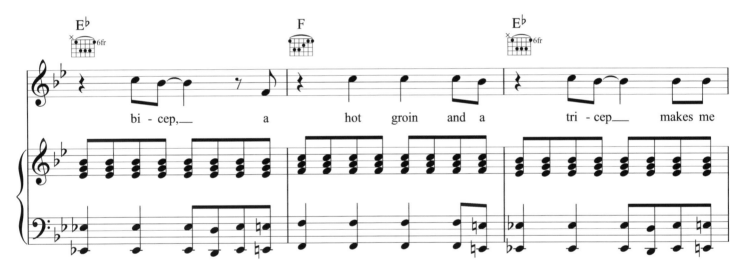

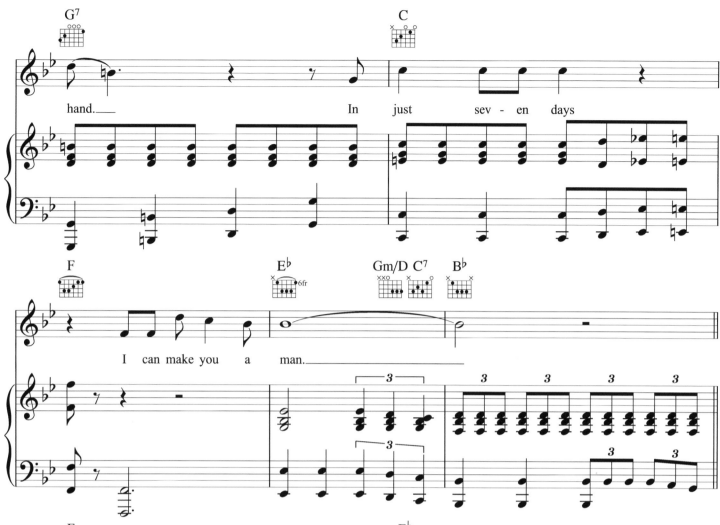

hand._____ In just sev - en days

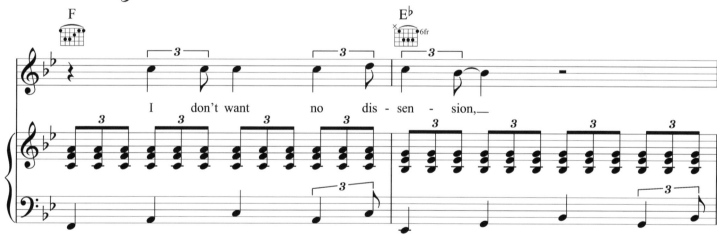

I can make you a man._____

I don't want no dis - sen - sion,

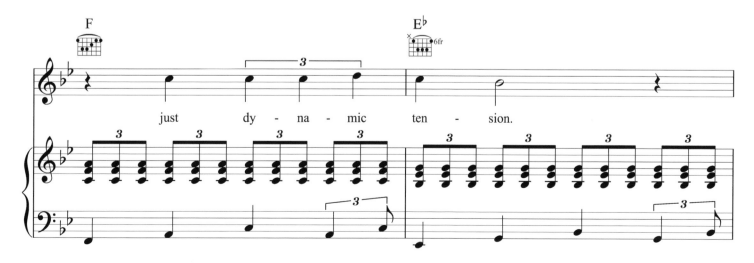

just dy - na - mic ten - sion.

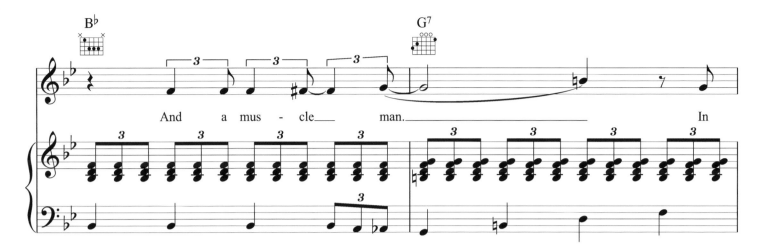

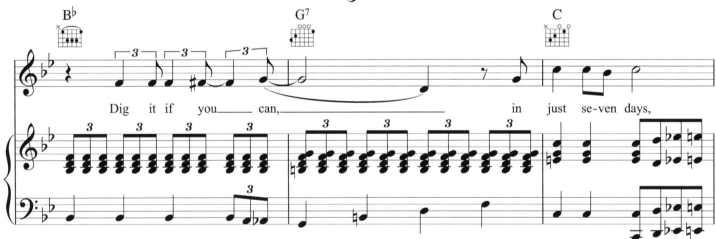

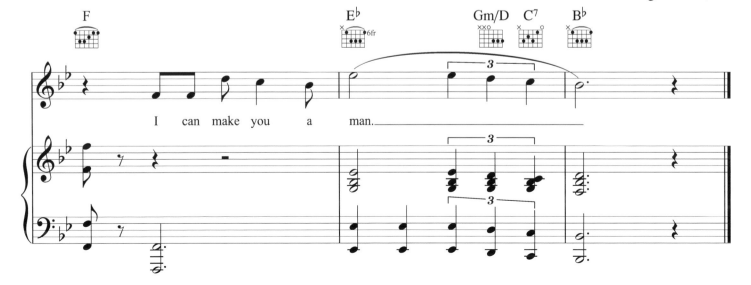

TOUCH-A TOUCH-A TOUCH-A TOUCH ME

WORDS & MUSIC BY RICHARD O'BRIEN

it on - ly leads to trou - ble and seat wet - ting.

2. Now all I want to know, is how to go,
3. Then if an - y - thing grows when you pose,

I've tast - ed blood and I want more. (More, more.)
I'll oil you up and rub you down. (Down, down.)

I'll put up no res - ist - ance, I want to stay the dis - tance,
And that's just one small frac - tion, of the main at - trac - tion,

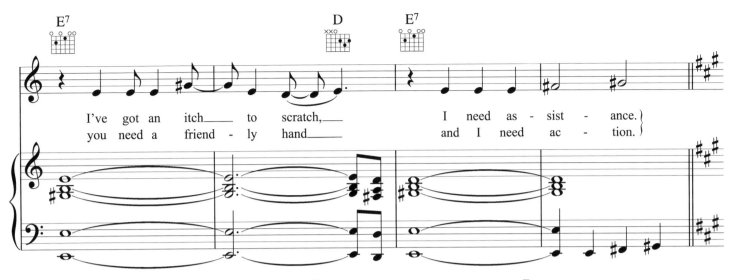

I've got an itch___ to scratch,___ I need as - sist - ance.
you need a friend - ly hand___ and I need ac - tion.

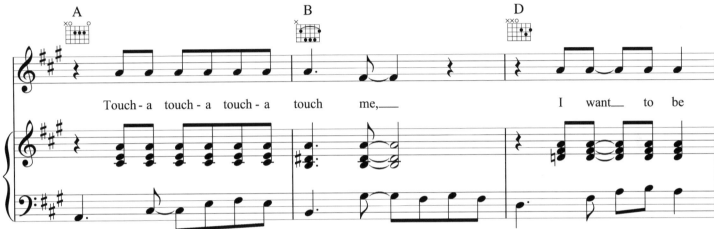

Touch - a touch - a touch - a touch me,___ I want___ to be

dirt - y,___ thrill me, chill me, ful - fil me,___

crea - ture of___ the night. night.

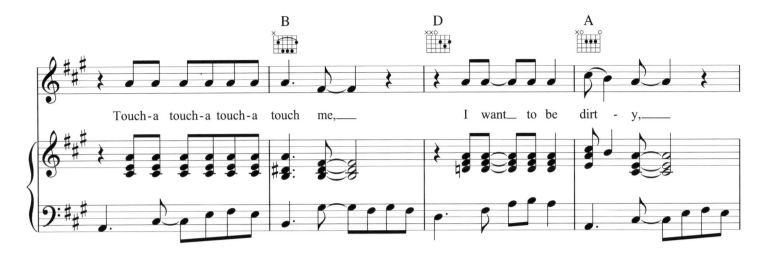

Touch-a touch-a touch-a touch me,___ I want___ to be dirt - y,___

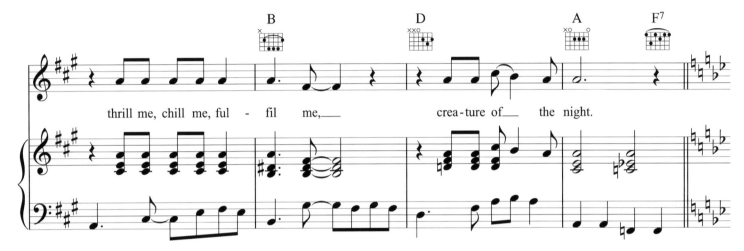

thrill me, chill me, ful - fil me,___ crea-ture of___ the night.

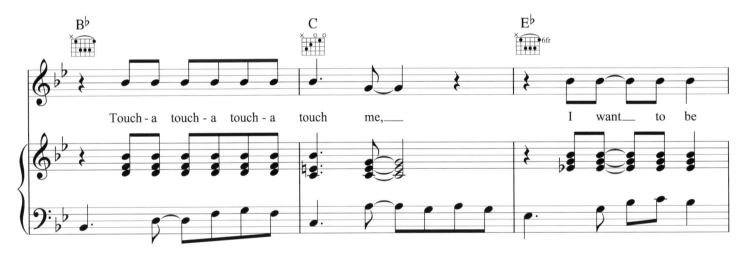

Touch-a touch-a touch-a touch me,___ I want___ to be

dirt - y,___ thrill me, chill me, ful - fil me,___

crea - ture of____ the night, crea - ture of____ the

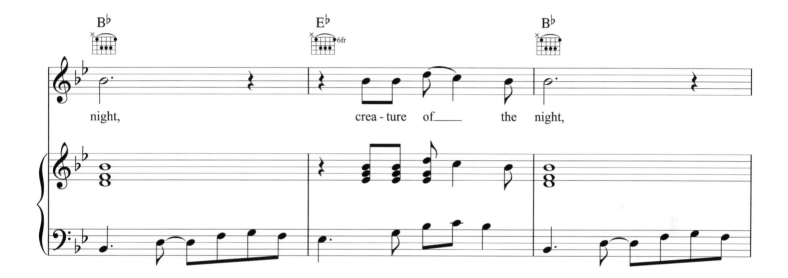

night, crea - ture of____ the night,

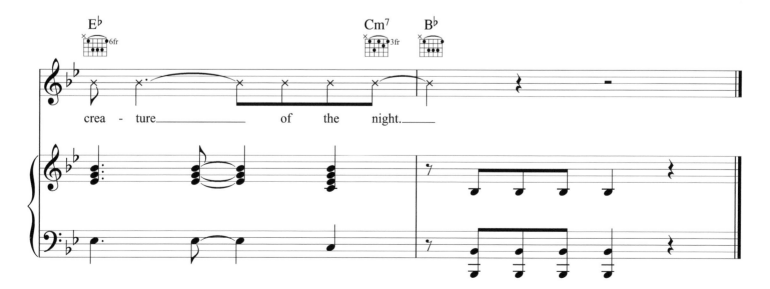

crea - ture____ of the night.____

ONCE IN A WHILE

WORDS & MUSIC BY RICHARD O'BRIEN

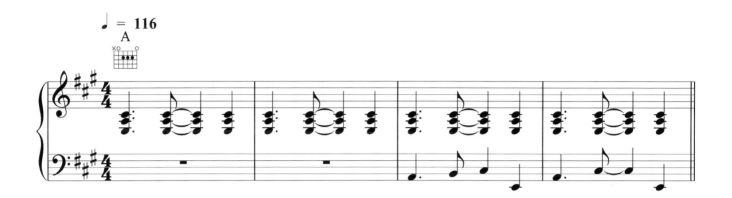

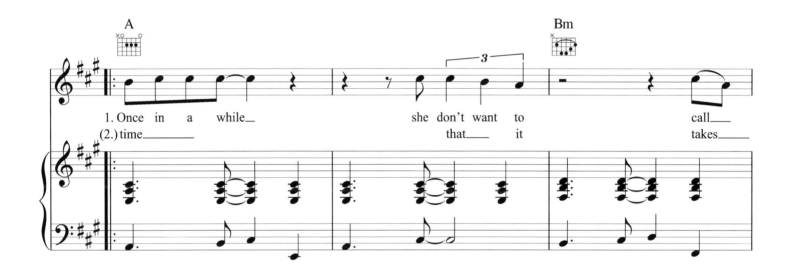

1. Once in a while she don't want to call

(2.) time that it takes

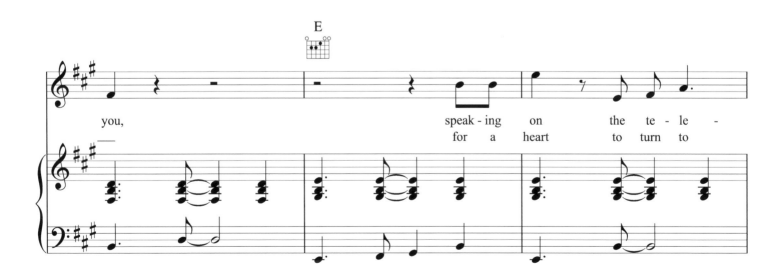

you,

speak-ing on the te - le -

for a heart to turn to

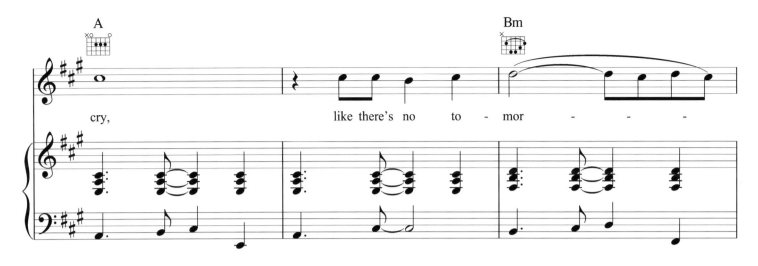

cry, like there's no to - mor - - - -

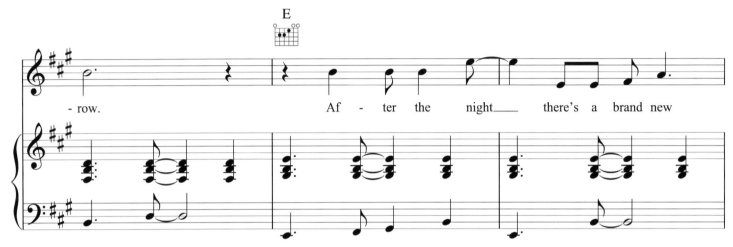

- row. Af - ter the night___ there's a brand new

day,___ and there'll be no pain,

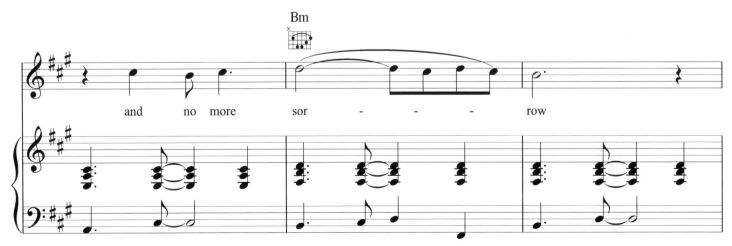

and no more sor - - - row

so wash your face, and phone

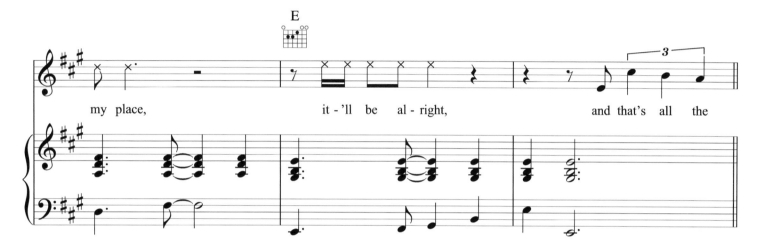

my place, it-'ll be al-right, and that's all the

time that it takes

for a heart to

beat a-gain. So give me a sign,

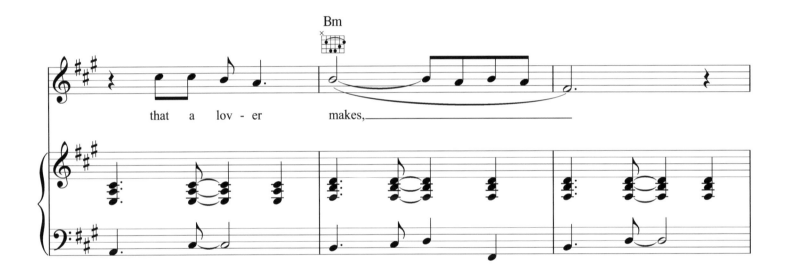

that a lov-er makes,_____

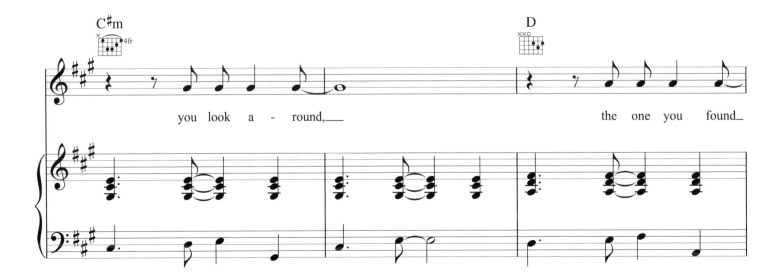

you look a-round,___ the one you found___

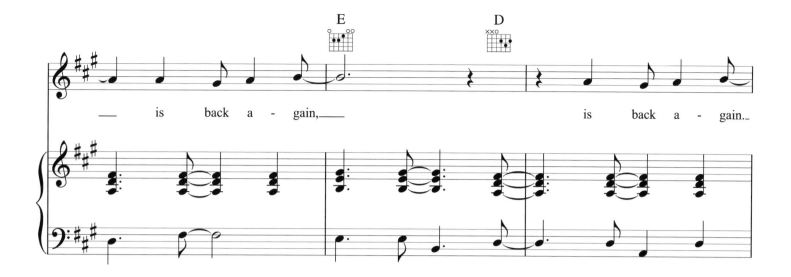

is back a - gain, _____ is back a - gain..

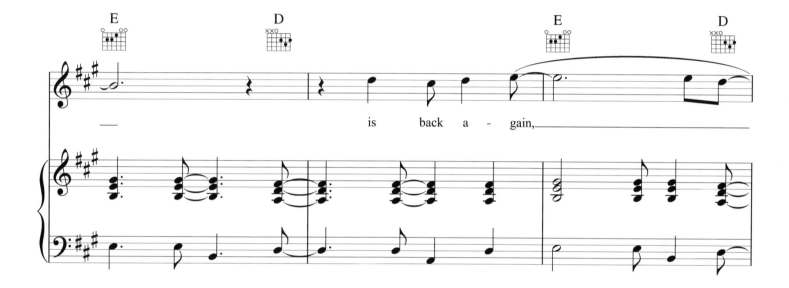

is back a - gain, _____

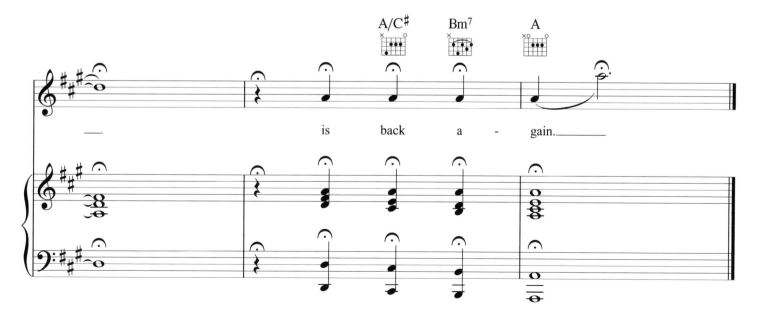

is back a - gain. _____

EDDIE'S TEDDY

WORDS & MUSIC BY RICHARD O'BRIEN

bike,
reads:
shoot-ing up junk.
"I'm out of my head,

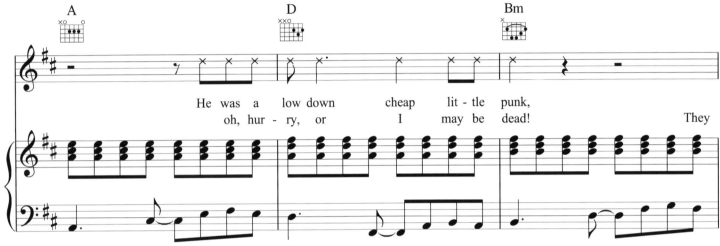

He was a low down cheap lit - tle punk,
oh, hur - ry, or I may be dead!
They

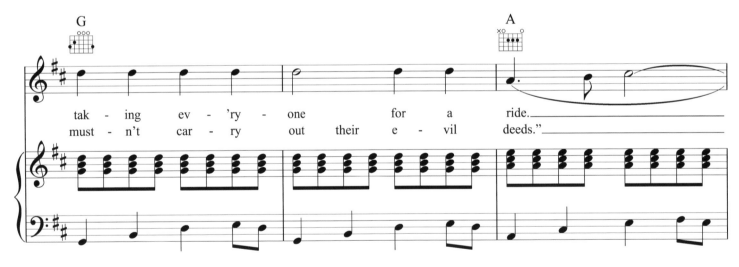

tak - ing ev - 'ry - one for a ride.____
must - n't car - ry out their e - vil deeds."____

When Ed - die said he did - n't like his ted - dy, you knew____

_____ he was a no good kid. _____ But when he threat-ened your life _____ with a

switch-blade knife. What a guy. Makes you cry. And I did.

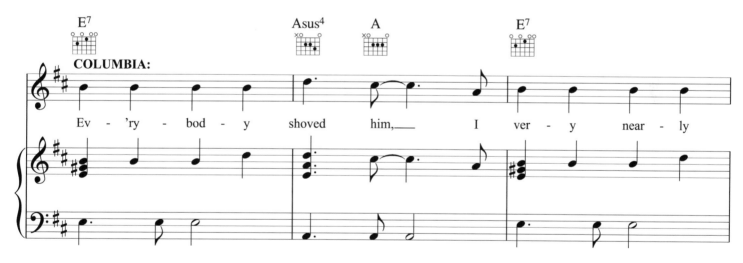

COLUMBIA: Ev-'ry-bod-y shoved him, _____ I ver-y near-ly

loved him, _____ I said, "Hey list-en to me, stay

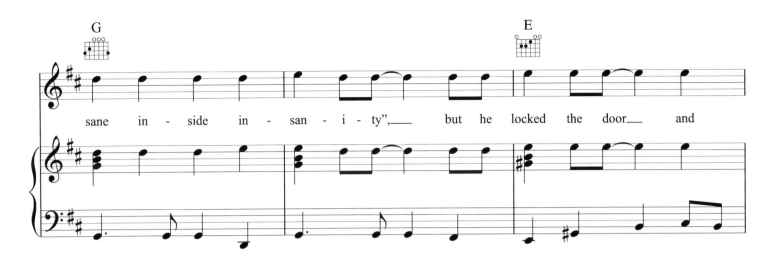

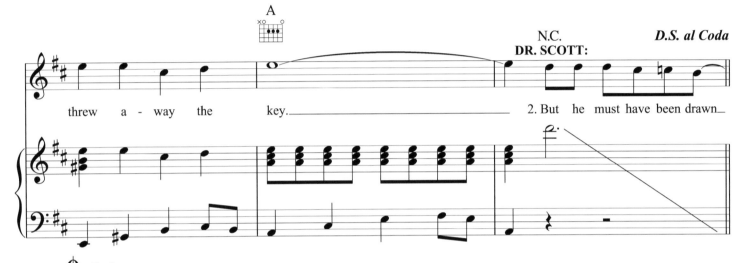

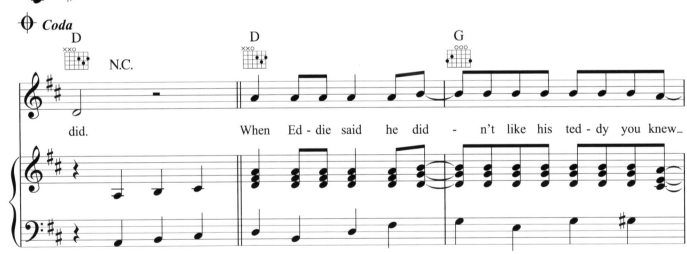

switch-blade knife, what a guy makes you cry and I did. Whoa, whoa, whoa. What a

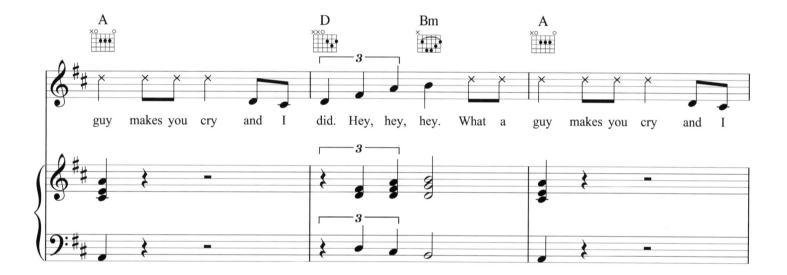

guy makes you cry and I did. Hey, hey, hey. What a guy makes you cry and I

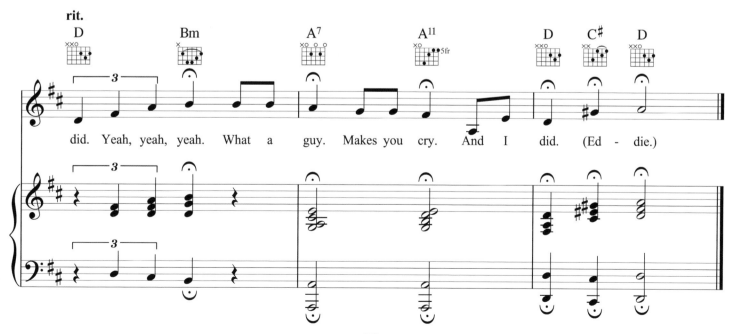

did. Yeah, yeah, yeah. What a guy. Makes you cry. And I did. (Ed - die.)

PLANET SCHMANET

WORDS & MUSIC BY RICHARD O'BRIEN

a men - tal mind - fuck can be nice._____ You'd bet - ter

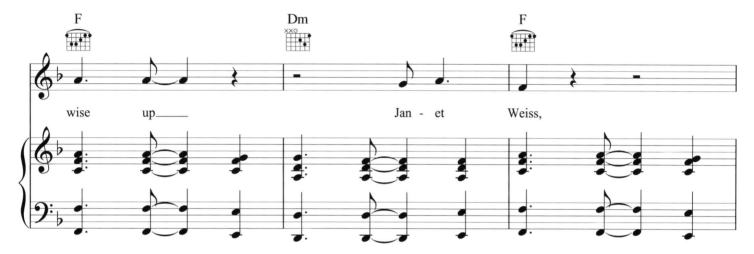

wise up_____ Jan - et Weiss,

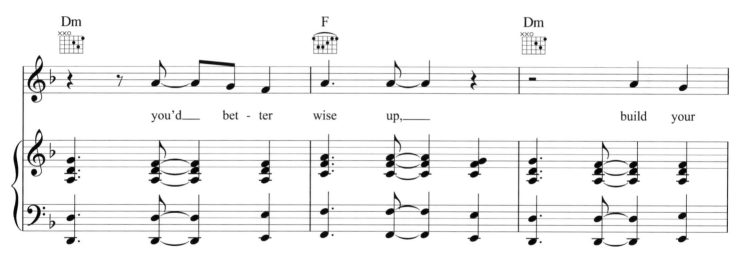

you'd___ bet - ter wise up,_____ build your

thighs up, you'd___ bet - ter wise up._____ And then she

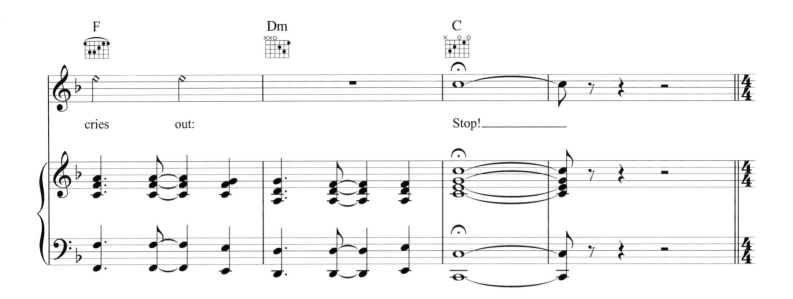

cries out: Stop!_____

♩ = 84

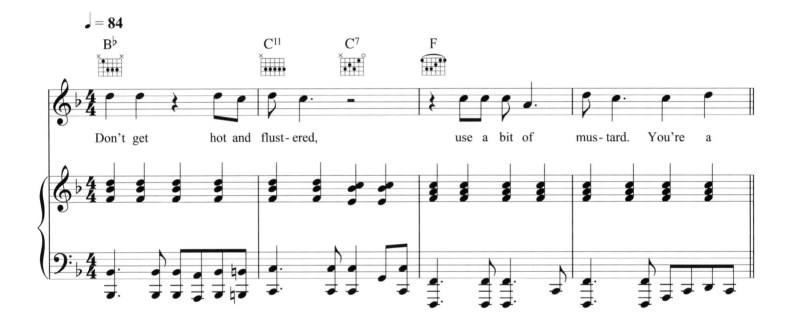

Don't get hot and flust- ered, use a bit of mus- tard. You're a

Repeat to fade

hot dog but you'd bet- ter not try to hurt___ her, Frank- fur- ter. You're a

FLOOR SHOW

WORDS & MUSIC BY RICHARD O'BRIEN

COLUMBIA: 1. It was great when it all be-gan,_____ I was a
(2.) just sev-en hours_____ old_____ and tru-ly

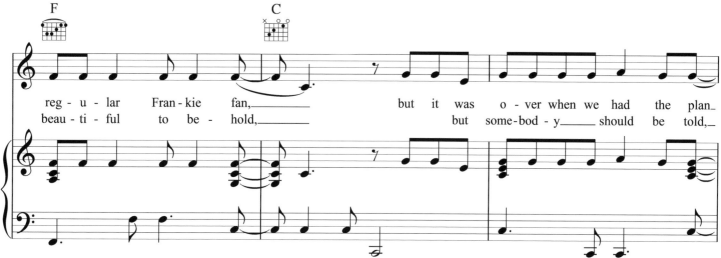

reg-u-lar Fran-kie fan,_____ but it was o-ver when we had the plan_
beau-ti-ful to be-hold,_____ but some-bod-y_____ should be told,_

to start work-ing on a mus-cle man.___ Now the
my li-bi-do has-n't been___ con-trolled. Now the

on-ly thing that gives me hope___ is my love of a cer-tain dope.___
on-ly thing I've come to trust___ is an or-gas-mic rush of lust.___

Rose tints my world, keeps me safe from my trou-ble and pain.___
Rose tints my world, keeps me safe from my trou-ble and pain.___

1.

ROCKY: 2. I'm

2.

BRAD: It's be -

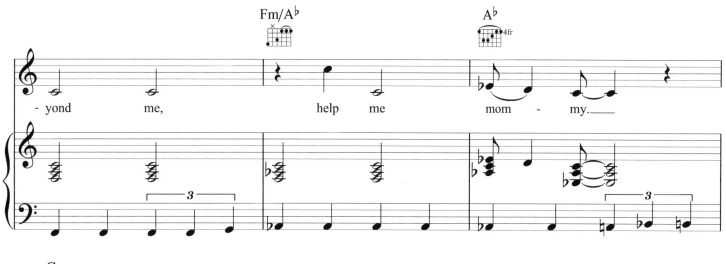

-yond me, help me mom - my.___

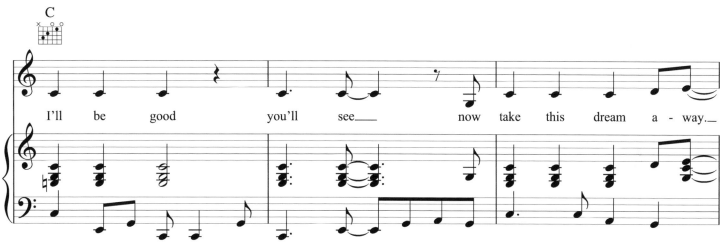

I'll be good you'll see___ now take this dream a - way.___

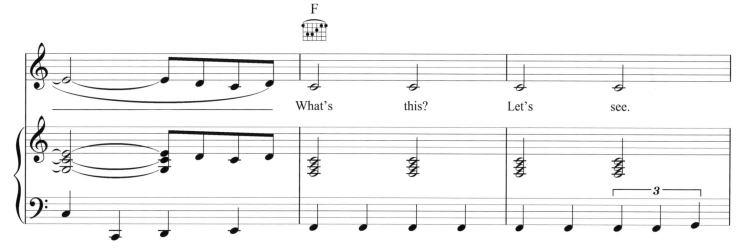

___ What's this? Let's see.

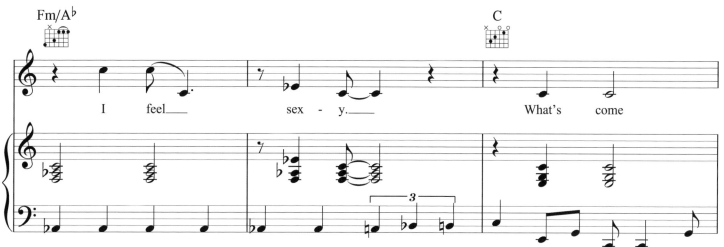

I feel___ sex - y.___ What's come

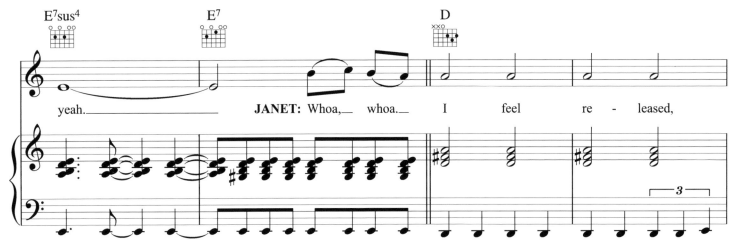

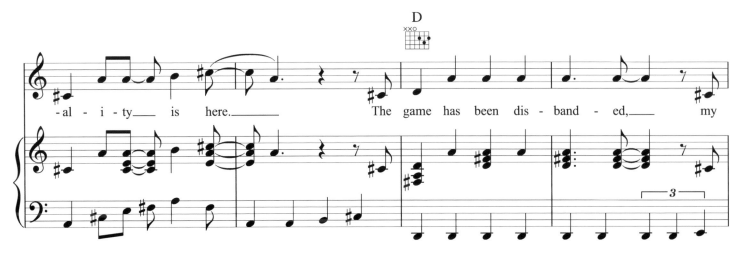

mind has been___ ex - pand - ed,___ it's a gas that Frank - y's land - ed,___ his

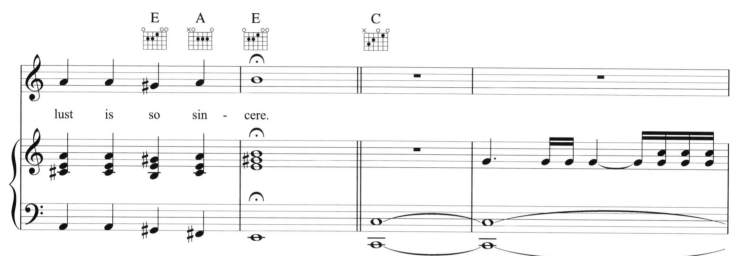

lust is so sin - cere.

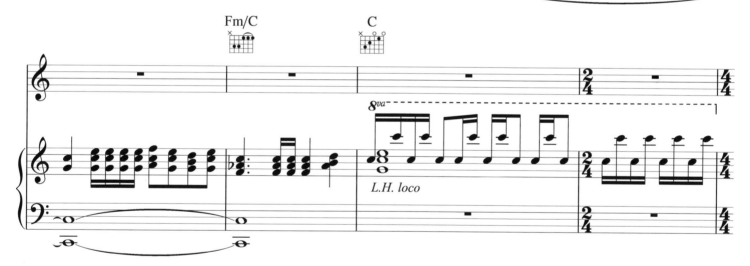

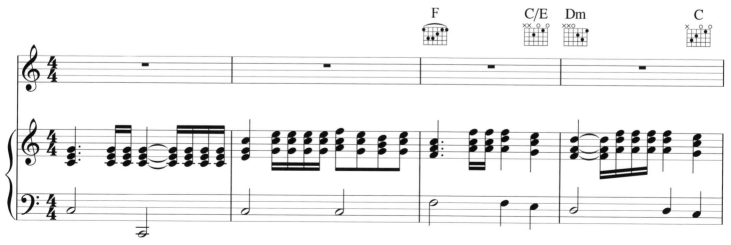

swim the warm wa-ters of sins of the flesh, e-ro-tic night-mares___ be-

-yond an-y mea-sure and sen-sual day-dreams to trea-sure___ for-ev-er.

Can't you just see it,___ whoa, oh, oh.

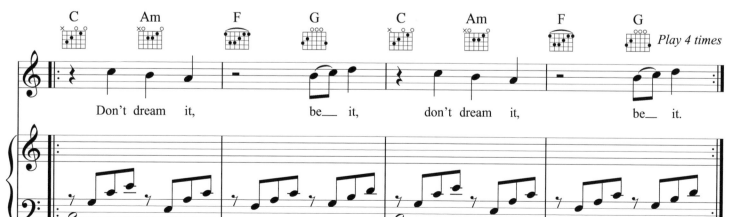

Don't dream it, be___ it, don't dream it, be___ it.

Play 4 times

hit and your mind goes ping! Your heart-'ll thump and your blood will sing so let the

par - ty and the sounds rock on.___ I'm gon - na shake it till the life has gone,_

rose tint my world, keep me safe from my trou - ble and pain.___

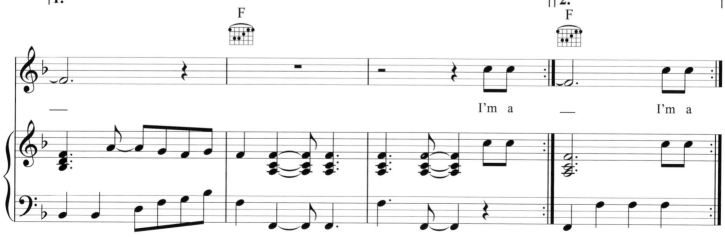

I'm a ___ I'm a

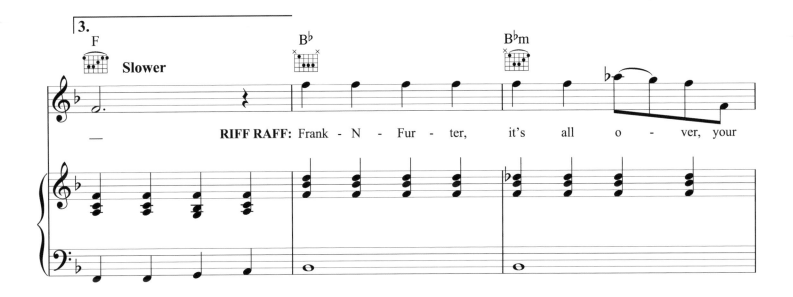

Slower

RIFF RAFF: Frank - N - Fur - ter, it's all o - ver, your

mis - sion is a fail - ure, your life-style's too ex - treme.____ I'm your new com-mand - er,

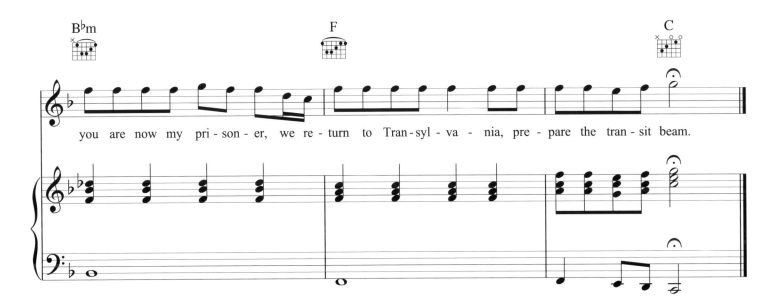

you are now my pri - son - er, we re - turn to Tran-syl - va - nia, pre - pare the tran - sit beam.

I'M GOING HOME

WORDS & MUSIC BY RICHARD O'BRIEN

1. On the day I went a-way, good-bye was all I had to
2. Ev-'ry-where I went it's been the same feel-ing, like I'm out-side

say, now I, I want to come a-gain and stay oh my,
in the rain. Wheel-ing free to try and find a game, deal-

my.____ Smile____ and that will mean I may._____
-ing____ cards for sor - row, cards for pain._____

'Cause I've seen, I've seen blue skies____ through the

tears____ in my eyes,____ in my eyes,____ and I

re - al - ise I'm go - ing

home.

I'm go - ing

1.

home.

2.

I'm go - ing

home,⎯⎯⎯⎯

I'm go - ing home.

SUPER HEROES

WORDS & MUSIC BY RICHARD O'BRIEN

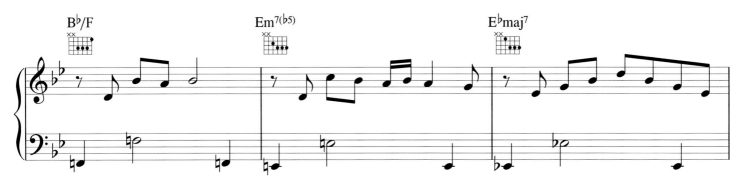

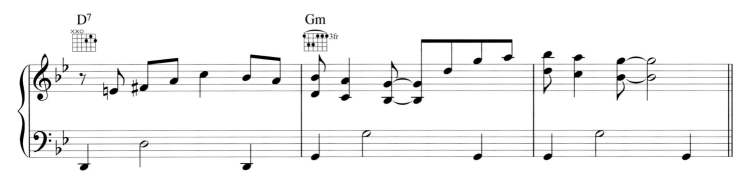

BRAD: 1. I've done a - lot,   God knows I've tried,__   to find the truth,   I've

JANET: 2. And su - per he - roes   come to feast,__   to taste the flesh

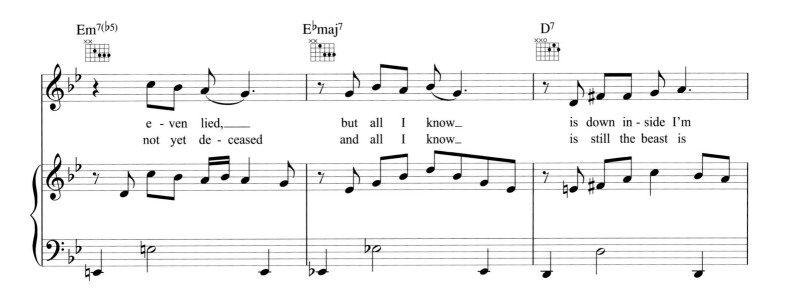

e - ven lied,_____ but all I know_____ is down in - side I'm
not yet de - ceased and all I know_____ is still the beast is

bleed - ing._____ Ooh._____
feed - ing._____

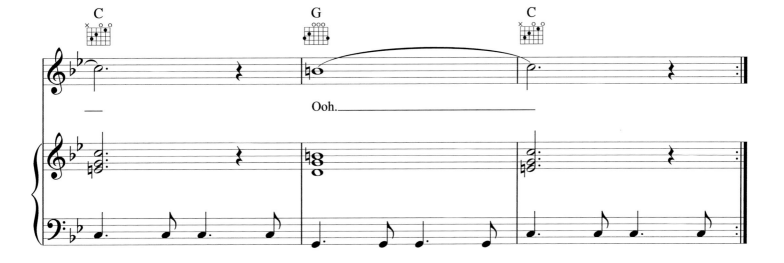

Ooh._____

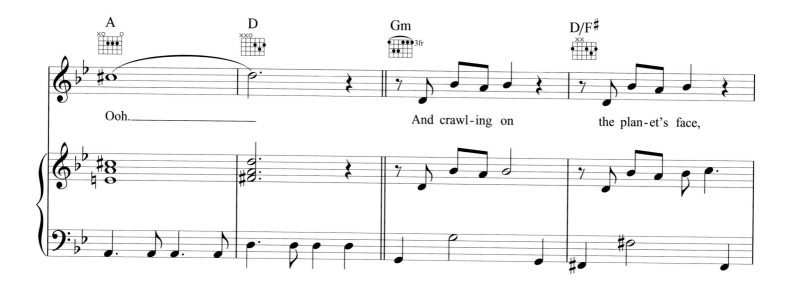

Ooh._____ And crawl-ing on the plan-et's face,

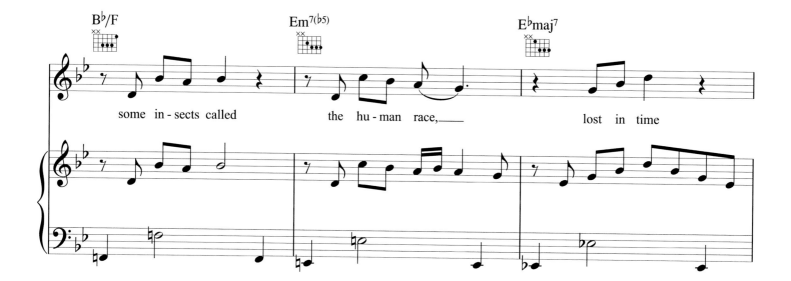

some in-sects called the hu-man race,_____ lost in time

and lost in space and___ mean - ing._____ (Mean - ing.)___

SCIENCE FICTION – DOUBLE FEATURE: REPRISE

WORDS & MUSIC BY RICHARD O'BRIEN

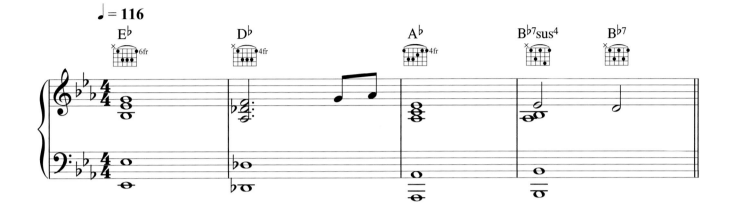

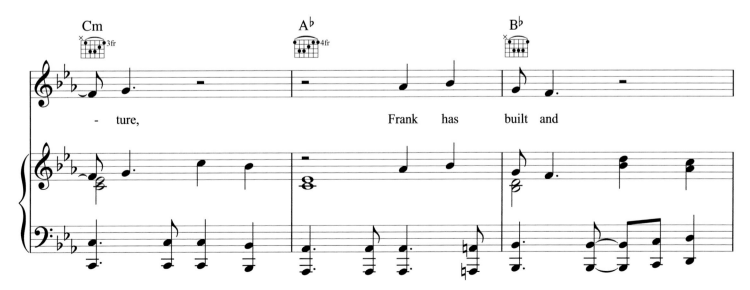

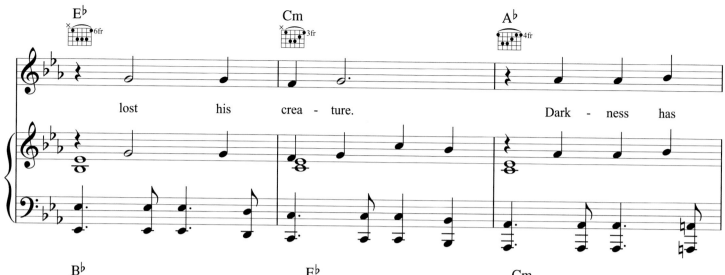

lost his crea - ture. Dark - ness has

con - quered Brad and Ja - net,

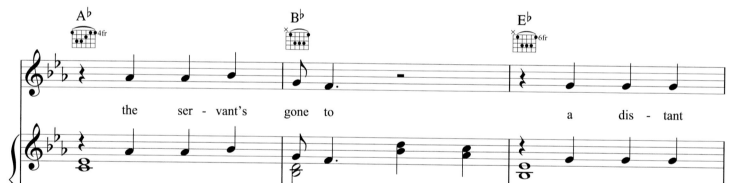

the ser - vant's gone to a dis - tant

plan - et, oh, oh, oh, oh._____ At the